ANIMAL RECORD BREAKERS

CHINESE SALAMANDER

THE LARGEST AMPHIBIAN

RACHAEL MORLOCK

PowerKiDS press
New York

Published in 2020 by The Rosen Publishing Group, Inc.
29 East 21st Street, New York, NY 10010

First Edition

Editor: Theresa Emminizer
Book Design: Reann Nye

Photo Credits: Series Art (frame) HiSunnySky/Shutterstock.com; Series Art (Banners) Roberto Castillo/Shutterstock.com; Series Art (background) Wilqkuku/Shutterstock.com; Cover, pp. 5, 9 (Chinese giant salamander), 13, 15, 17, 22 tristan tan/Shutterstock.com; p. 7 GOH CHAI HIN/AFP/Getty Images; p. 9 (Japanese Giant salamander) Martin Voeller/Shutterstock.com; p. 9 (hellbender salamander) https://commons.wikimedia.org/wiki/File:Hellbender.jpg; p. 11 © istockphoto.com/photo_m; p. 19 Zhuo zhongwei/AP Images; p. 21 GOH CHAI HIN/AFP/Getty Images.

Cataloging-in-Publication Data

Names: Morlock, Rachael.
Title: Chinese salamander: the largest amphibian / Rachael Morlock.
Description: New York : PowerKids Press, 2020. | Series: Animal record breakers | Includes glossary and index.
Identifiers: ISBN 9781725308664 (pbk.) | ISBN 9781725308688 (library bound) | ISBN 9781725308671 (6 pack)
Subjects: LCSH: Chinese giant salamander–Juvenile literature.
Classification: LCC QL668.C24 M667 2020 | DDC 597.8'5–dc23

Manufactured in the United States of America

CPSIA Compliance Information: Batch #CWPK20. For Further Information contact Rosen Publishing, New York, New York at 1-800-237-9932.

CONTENTS

LIVING FOSSILS

If you came across a Chinese giant salamander, you might think it belonged to another world. Its body is long, bumpy, mud-colored, and flat with four stubby limbs. Tiny eyes peer out from its head. But this amphibian isn't from another world, it's from another time.

Scientists call the Chinese salamander a living **fossil**. That's because it has hardly changed for millions of years. Chinese salamanders reach a record-breaking size, and they've lived on Earth since the time of the dinosaurs.

Chinese salamanders are amphibians, like frogs, toads, and newts. They are cold-blooded and have a bony skeleton and slimy skin.

UNUSUALLY LARGE

The Chinese salamander tops the charts as the largest amphibian in the world. These giants have been known to grow almost 6 feet (1.8 m) long! Their tails make up more than half of their body length.

Large and powerful, Chinese salamanders are a top predator in the mountain streams where they live. To reach their great size, they eat fish, bugs, crayfish, snakes, turtles, snails, and other amphibians. They can weigh about 110 pounds (50 kg).

ANIMAL ACTION

Because of hunting and other threats, or dangers, few Chinese salamanders reach their full size in the wild anymore. Most only grow to about 3 feet (1 m) long.

The Chinese salamander's huge body is shaped like a cylinder, meaning it's long and rounded.

SALAMANDERS AROUND THE WORLD

Today, Chinese salamanders can be found in the Yangtze, Huang He, and Zhu Jiang Rivers in China. Although wild Chinese salamanders only live in China, they have two close family members in other parts of the world.

The Chinese salamander is the largest of three living members of the Cryptobranchidae family. The Japanese giant salamander is smaller and lives in Japan. The hellbender in North America is the smallest of the three. These giant salamanders have similar body shapes and **behaviors**.

MEASURING UP

CHINESE GIANT SALAMANDER
5.9 feet (1.8 m)

JAPANESE GIANT SALAMANDER
4.9 feet (1.5 m)

HELLBENDER SALAMANDER
2.4 feet (0.7 m)

All three large salamanders make a sticky slime that keeps predators away. Because of this ooze, the hellbender is sometimes called "snot otter."

LIFE OF A SALAMANDER

It can take a lifetime for a Chinese salamander to reach its full length. Despite its large size, each one begins life as a tiny egg. Salamanders grow from egg to larva to adult just as all amphibians do.

Every year, adult Chinese salamanders swim upstream toward fast-moving water with lots of **oxygen**. Males find an underwater cave to make a den. They push sand out of the den to prepare a space for **hatching** eggs. Then, they wait for a female.

A male who guards his cave from other males is called a den master. Females only enter the den to lay eggs.

EGGS TO LARVAE

A female can lay about 500 eggs at a time. Then, the male guards the eggs. He moves around to bring oxygen into the den, eats bad eggs, and keeps predators away.

The eggs hatch after about 60 days. The larvae look like tiny adult salamanders but with **gills**. They're about 1.2 inches (3 cm) long. The larvae can't eat on their own yet, so they have a special sack of fat attached to their bodies for food.

Male Chinese salamanders care for their young, but only until the eggs hatch. Then, the larvae leave the den.

GROWING AND CHANGING

After the first month, the larvae are ready to feed. They stay together in a group to hunt. The food they find helps them grow.

Chinese salamanders lose their gills when they are 8 or 9 inches (20 or 23 cm) long. Unlike other amphibians, they do not go through a complete **metamorphosis**. Their bodies grow, but their form doesn't change. The young salamanders separate from each other and live on their own. They usually become full adults at about five years old.

ANIMAL ACTION

Most amphibians grow underwater, then live mainly on land as adults. The Chinese Salamander is different. It spends most of its life below the surface of China's mountain streams.

When a Chinese salamander loses its gills, it can breathe underwater by taking in oxygen through its skin.

ADULT LIFE

As an adult, the Chinese salamander mainly lives on its own. It spends most days in underwater shelters. At night, it swims out to find food.

The Chinese salamander's small, lidless eyes can't see very well. Its nose and bumps on its skin help it sense movement nearby. Instead of actively hunting, it lies in wait for **prey** to pass. At the right moment, it opens its jaws wide to suck in water and prey, then snaps them shut again.

ANIMAL ACTION

Camouflage helps the Chinese salamander keep out of sight. Its spotted brown, gray, or green skin blends in with the rocky and muddy floor of its river home.

Chinese salamanders stay still or move slowly to save their strength. This way, they can go for long periods without eating.

RIVER HOMES

The Chinese salamander is most comfortable in water, though it's able to walk and breathe on land for short periods. Short legs with four toes in the front and five toes in the back help it walk. But its strong tail makes it better at swimming, and its smooth skin needs to stay wet.

Chinese salamanders need a clean river or stream in order to survive in the wild. They need cool, fresh water in forested, mountain **habitats**. Quick-flowing water is best.

ANIMAL ACTION

Scientists now believe that Chinese salamanders living in different rivers belong to different species, or groups. At least five species seem to have grown apart over time.

The Yangtze River in Yunnan Province, China, provides a home for wild salamanders. They also live in underground rivers.

THE STRUGGLE TO SURVIVE

Once a Chinese salamander is an adult, it's at the top of the animal food chain. Some giant salamanders in zoos have lived for 60 years. In the wild, this is less likely. Chinese salamanders are threatened by humans who hunt them for food and harm their homes.

Dams and **pollution** in rivers make it difficult for Chinese salamanders to survive. Hunting has reduced their numbers. As a result, Chinese salamanders are now endangered. This means they're close to dying out completely.

ANIMAL ACTION

Today it's illegal to catch wild Chinese salamanders, so farms raise different salamanders for meat. These animals sometimes escape or are let go. They can spread illnesses to wild salamanders.

In 2005, baby Chinese salamanders were released in Zhangjiajie, China, as part of an international effort to save the species.

SAVING SALAMANDERS

Chinese salamanders are running out of time, but it's not too late. Scientists are studying these animals to learn how to help them. Nature preserves in China provide safe habitats where Chinese salamanders can live. And people in some areas are removing harmful dams and protecting rivers from pollution.

The world's largest amphibian has lived on Earth for millions of years. Now humans must work to give it the best chance to survive in the years to come.

GLOSSARY

behavior: The way a person or animal acts.

camouflage: Colors or shapes on animals that allow them to blend in with their surroundings.

fossil: A trace, print, or the remains of an animal from a past age preserved in earth or rock.

gill: The body part that animals use to breathe in water.

habitat: The natural home for plants, animals, and other living things.

hatch: To break open or come out of.

metamorphosis: The process of change in the life cycle of some animals.

oxygen: A gas that is necessary for life.

pollution: When the environment is dirtied by waste, chemicals, and other harmful things.

prey: An animal hunted by other animals for food.

INDEX

WEBSITES

Due to the changing nature of Internet links, PowerKids Press has developed an online list of websites related to the subject of this book. This site is updated regularly. Please use this link to access the list: www.powerkidslinks.com/arb/salamander

TITLES IN THIS SERIES

GRL: M

ISBN: 9781725308664
6-pack ISBN: 9781725308671
9 781725 308664

PowerKiDS press

Listening to Leaders

Why Should I Listen to FIREFIGHTERS?

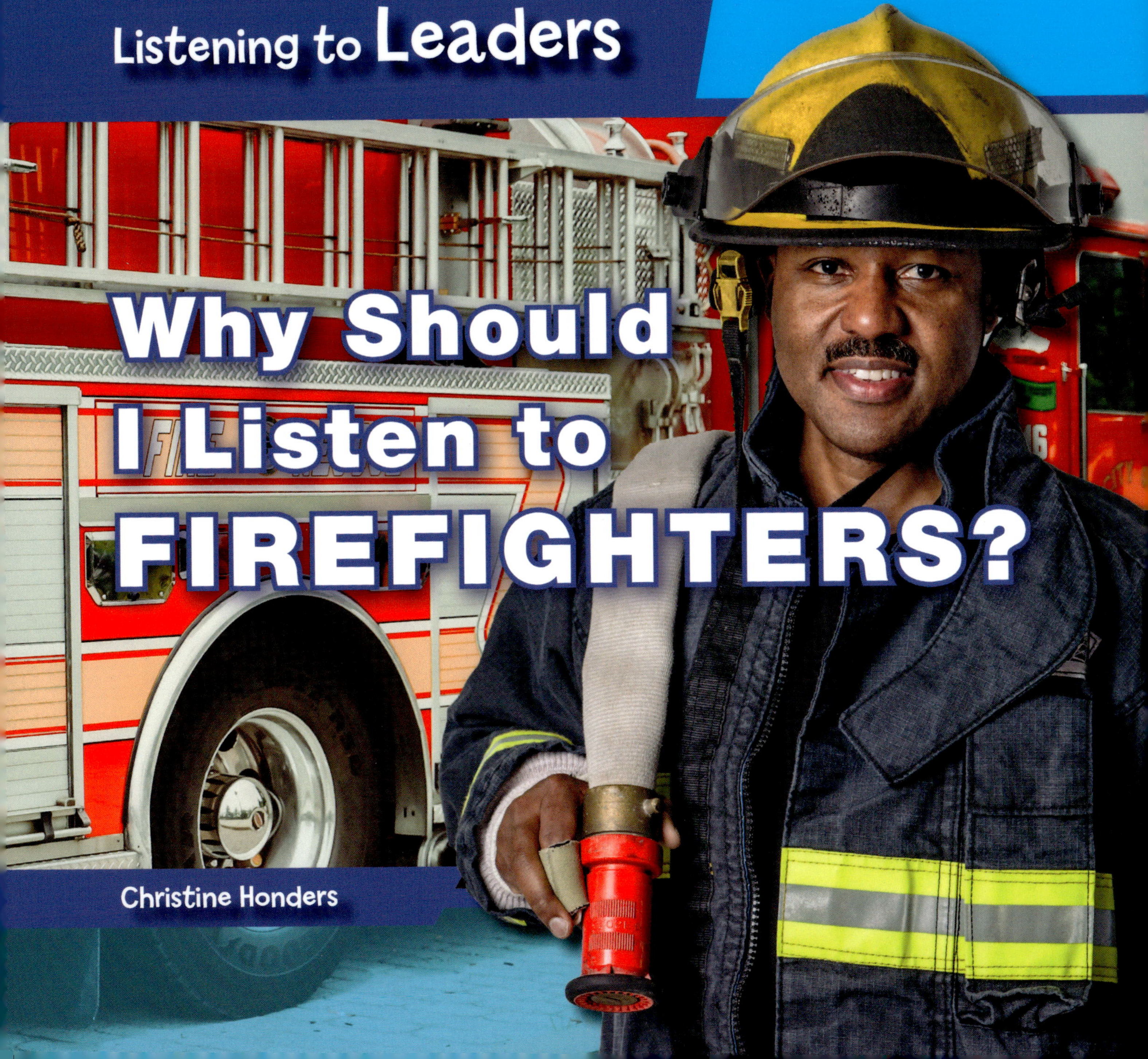

Christine Honders